Rescue Me Horses

A Touch of Gray

Cate Edwards

Travel Edition

Copywrite Cate Edwards/Little Thorns Books ©

All rights reserved. This book or any portion thereof may not be reproduced or used in any manner whatsoever without the express written permission of the publisher except for the use of brief notations in a book review. If you received this book as an ARC please note that digital copies are strictly for reviewers and may not be sold or redistributed. Littlethornsbooks@gmail.com

ISBN-13: 978-1975754068
ISBN-10:1975754069

A special thanks to my husband
Shawn....
for all the laughs and being my
best friend.

. Artist Note:
Please enjoy some extra
creations in the last pages from my other books.

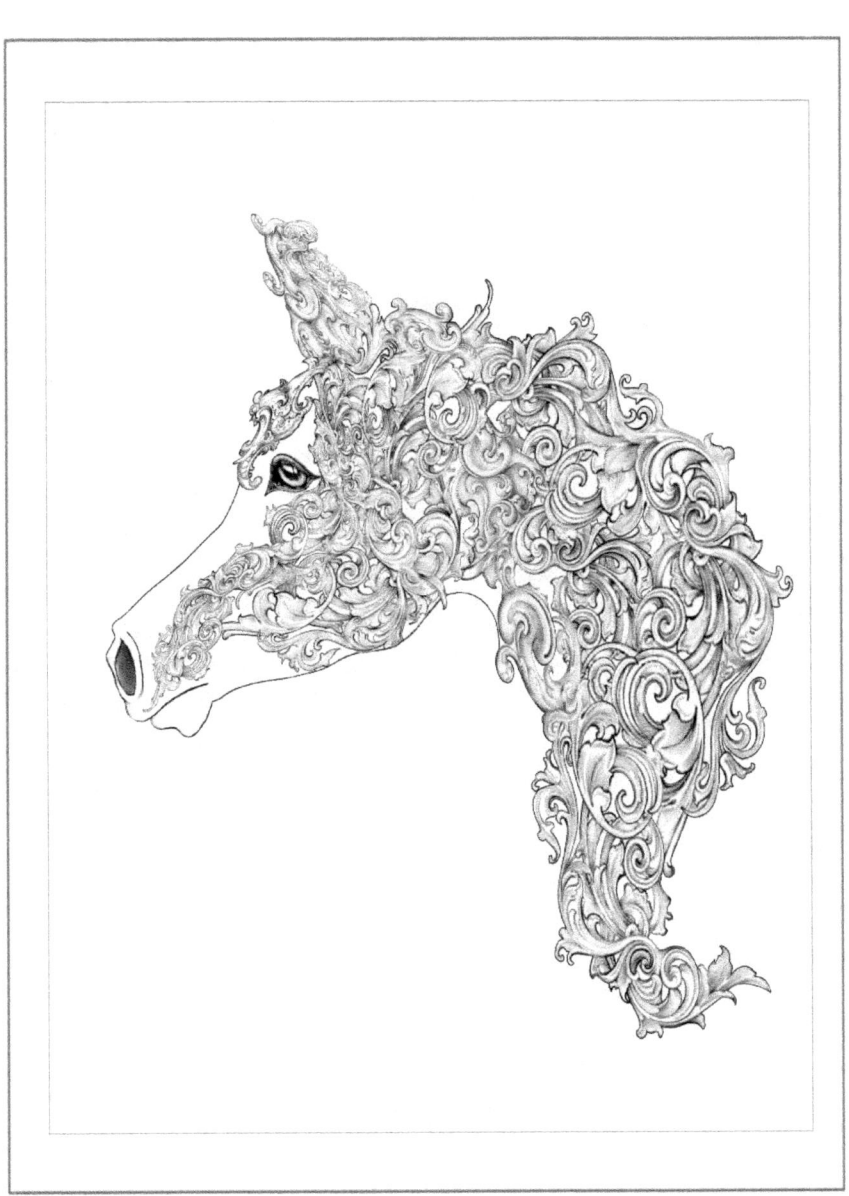

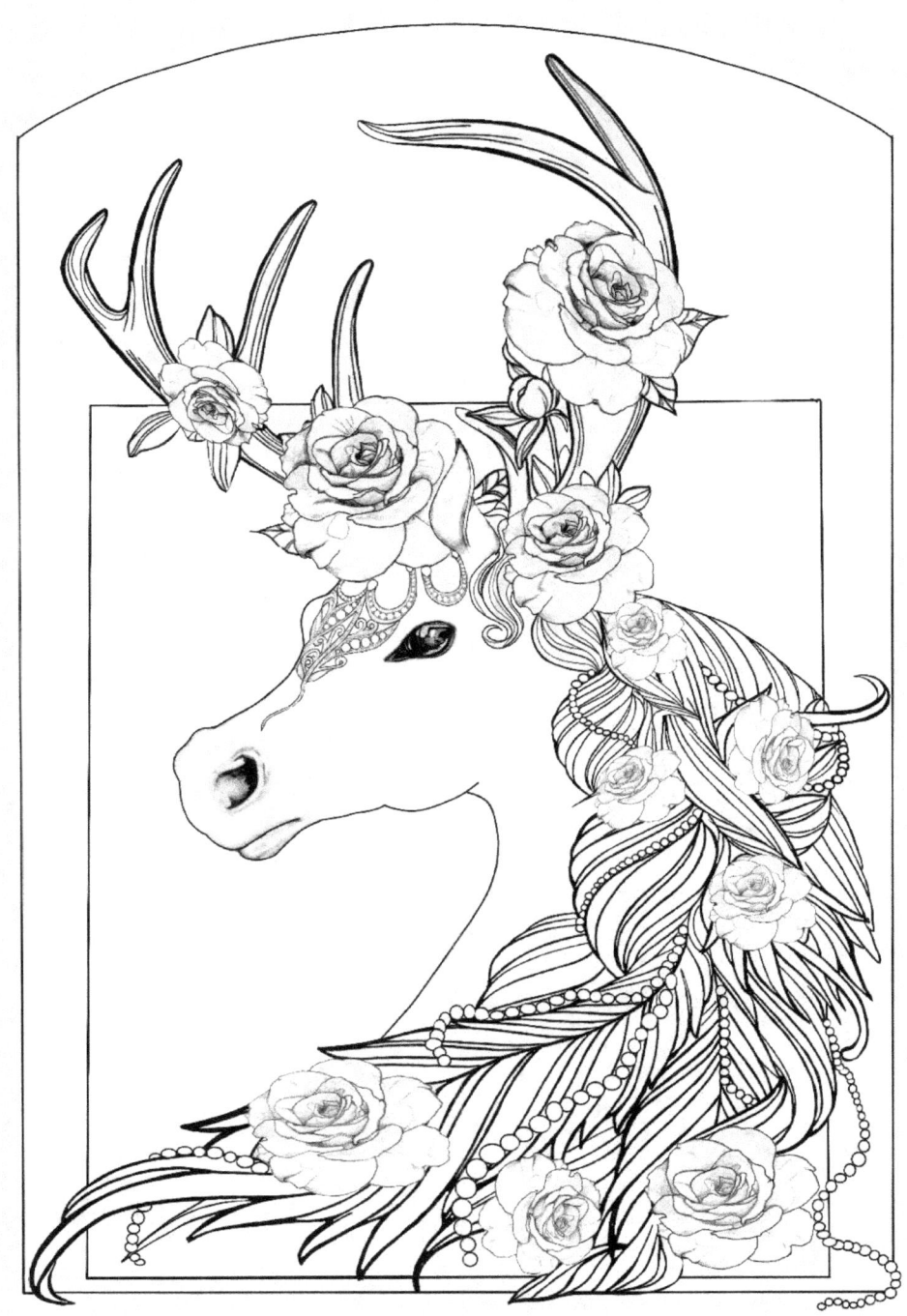

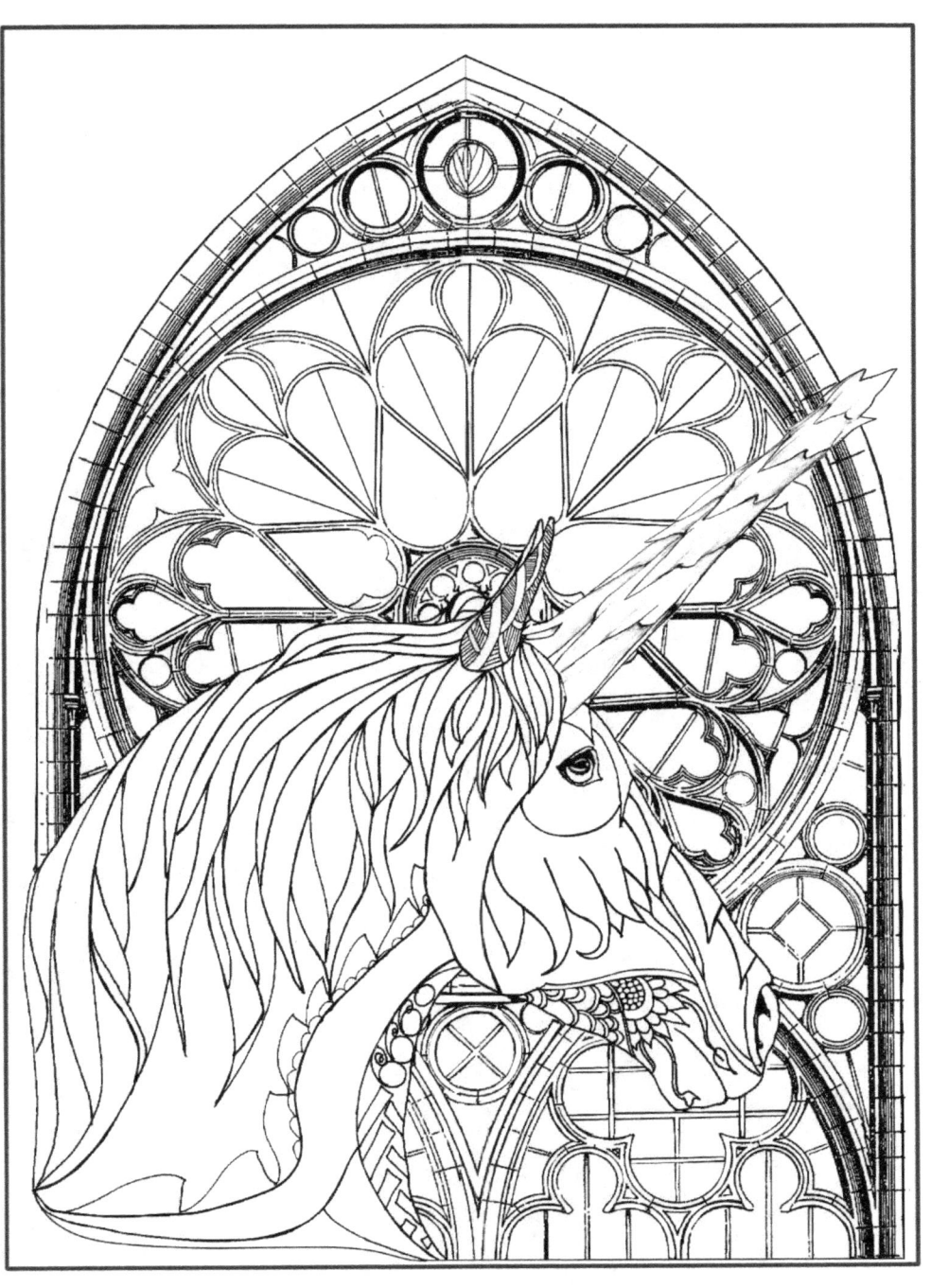

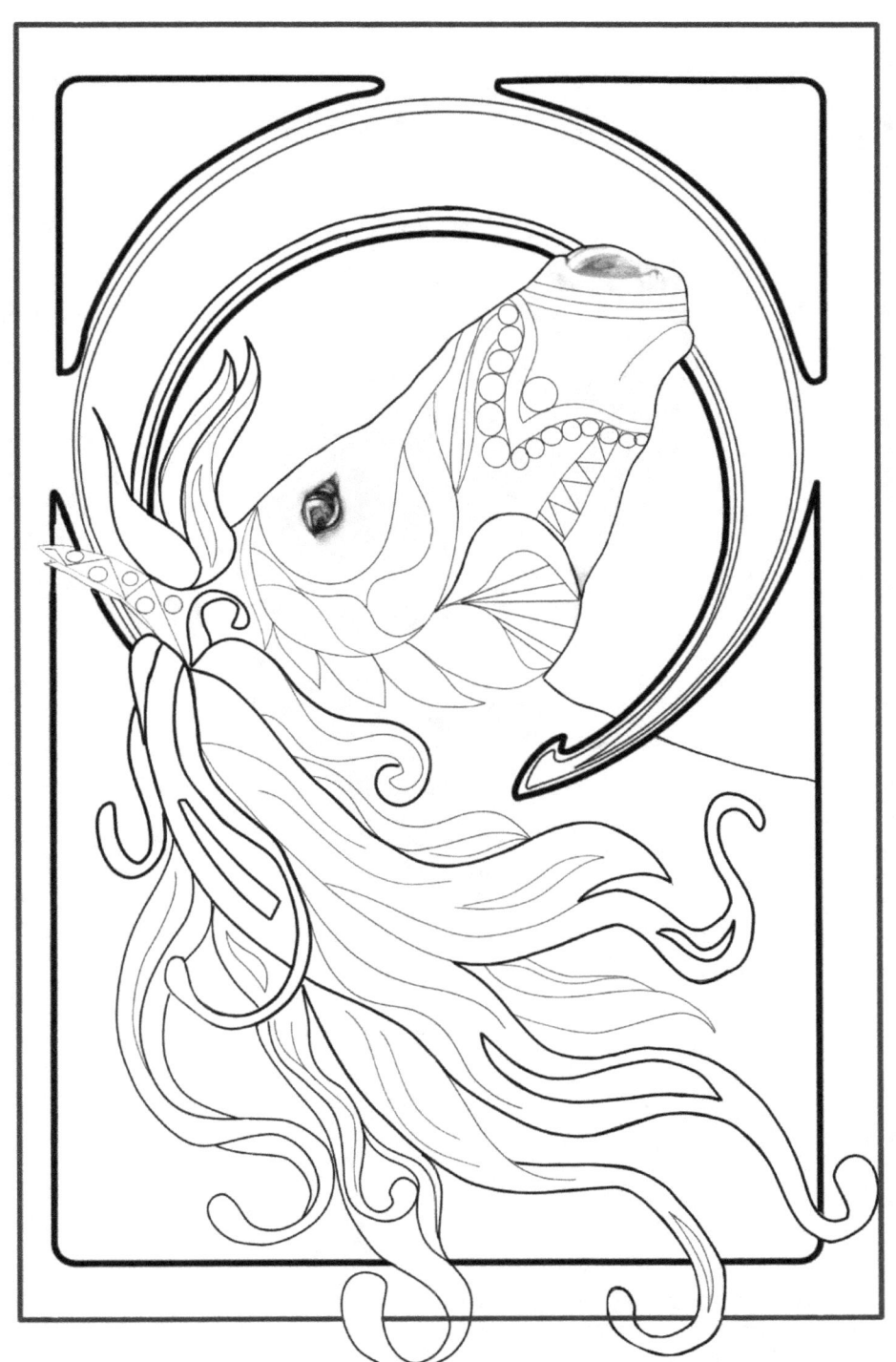

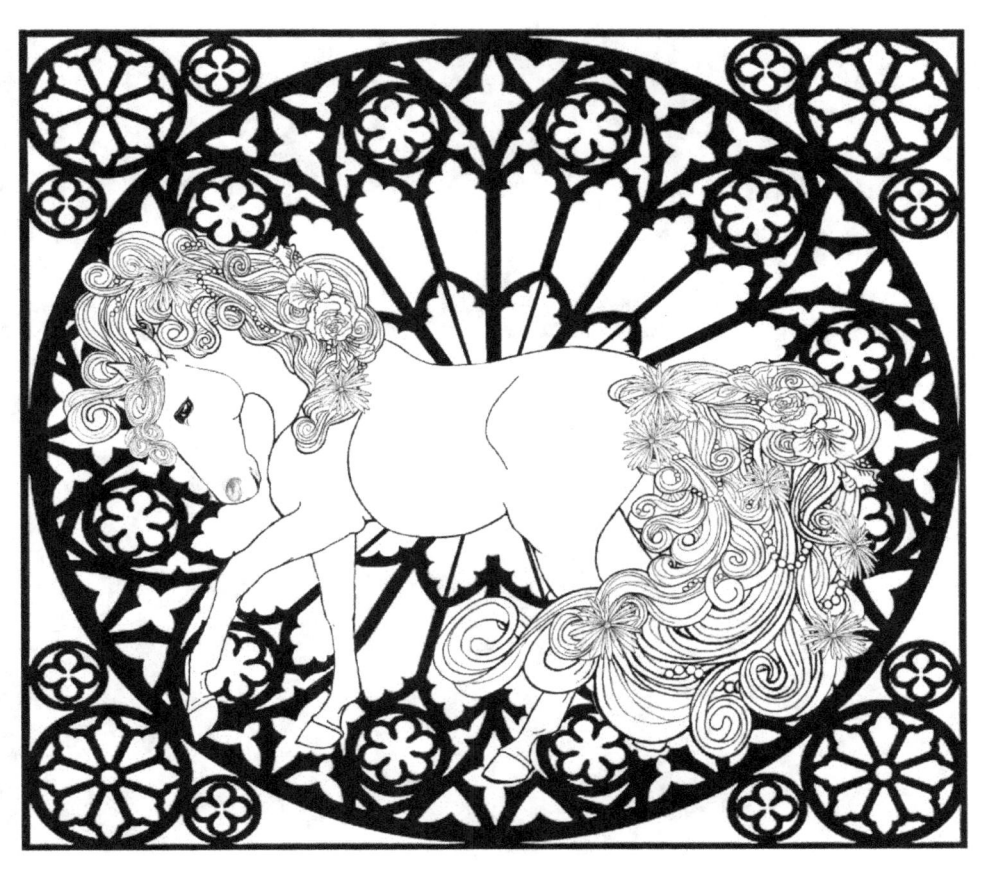

I always smile when I catch God looking at me through the eyes of a horse.

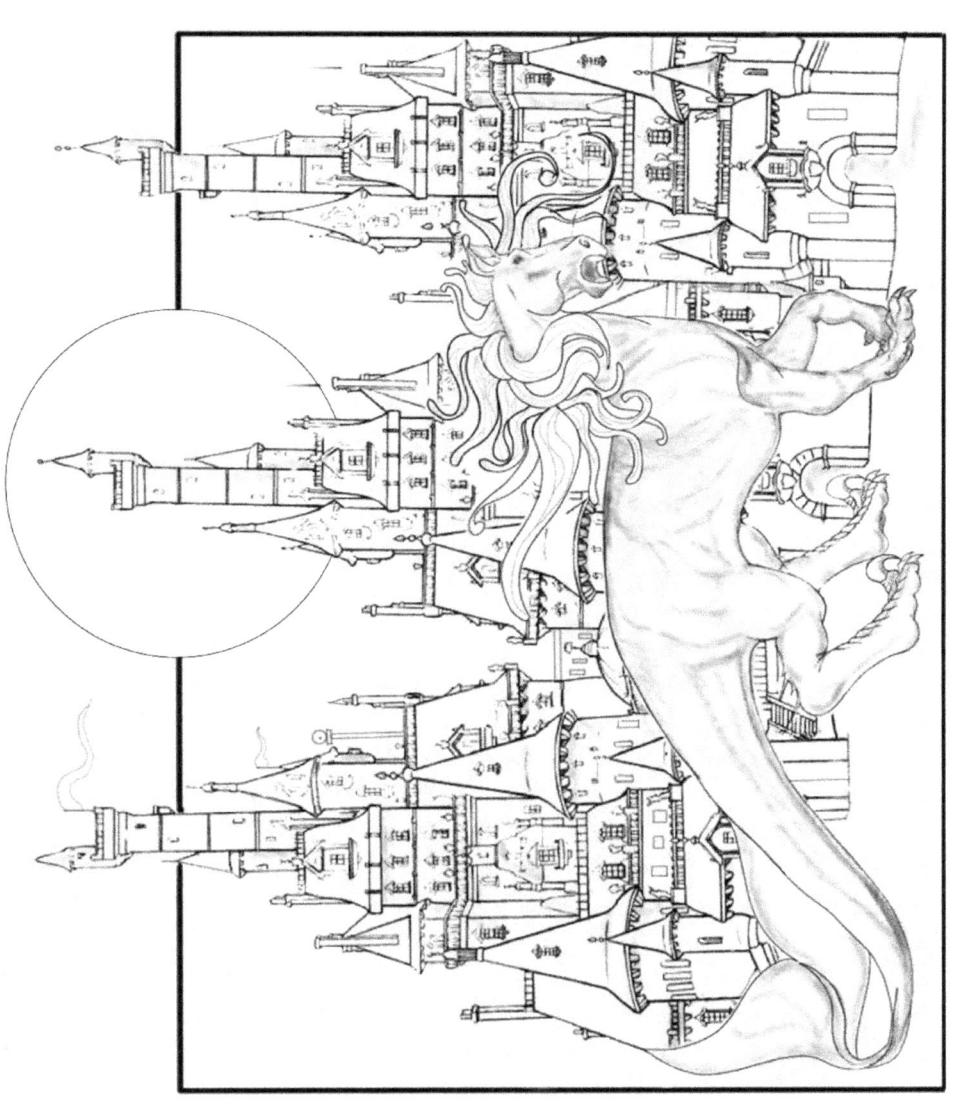

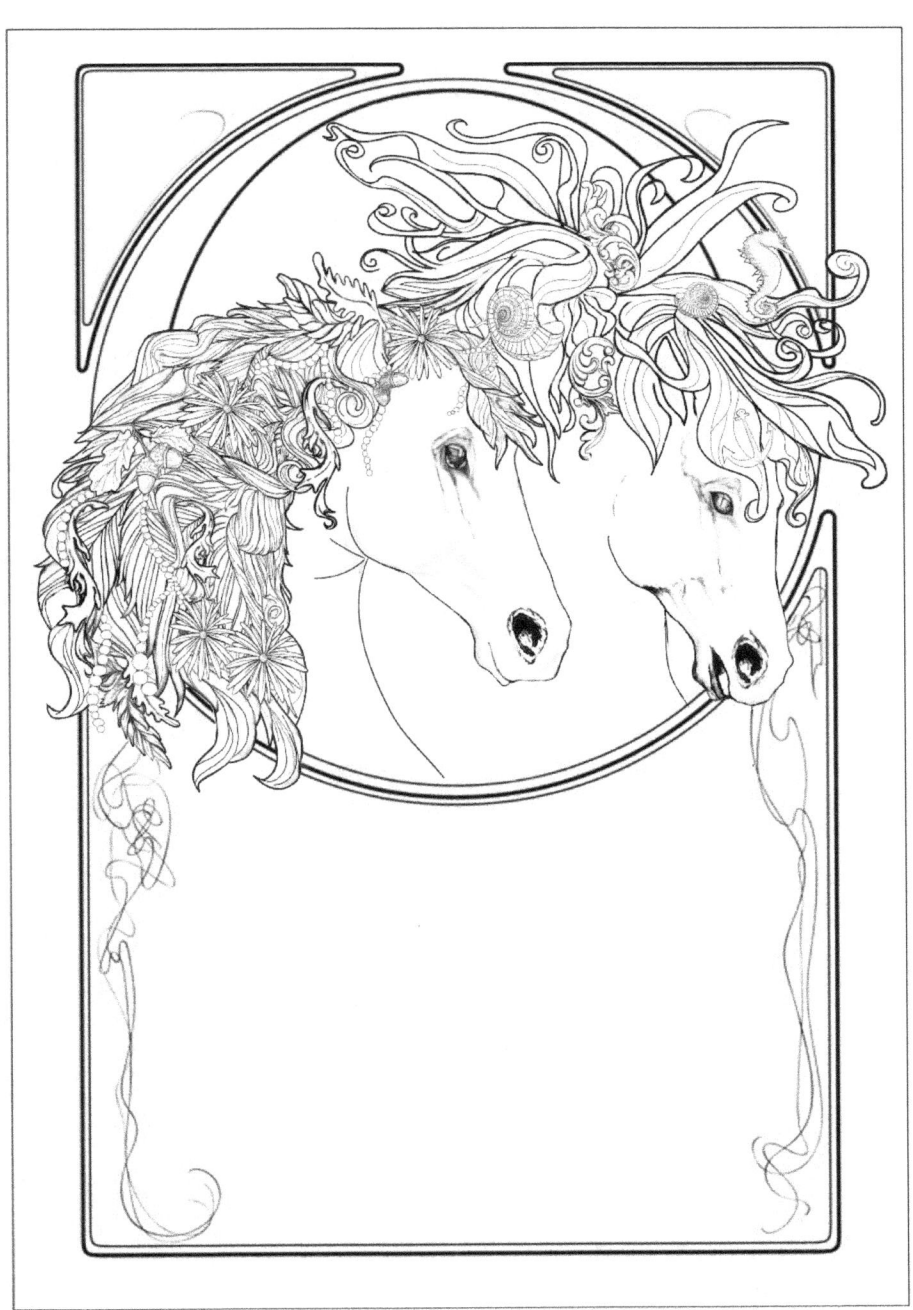

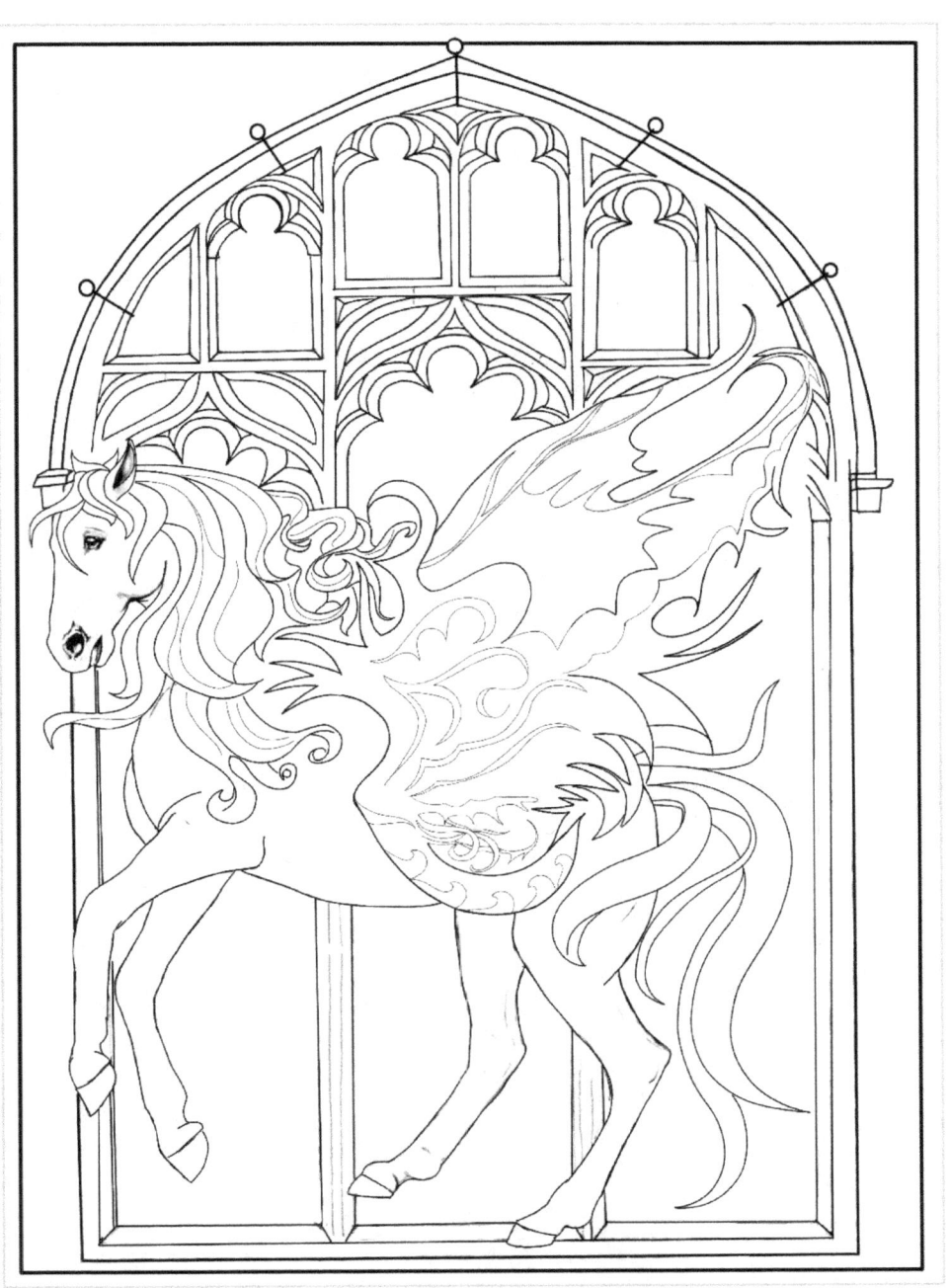

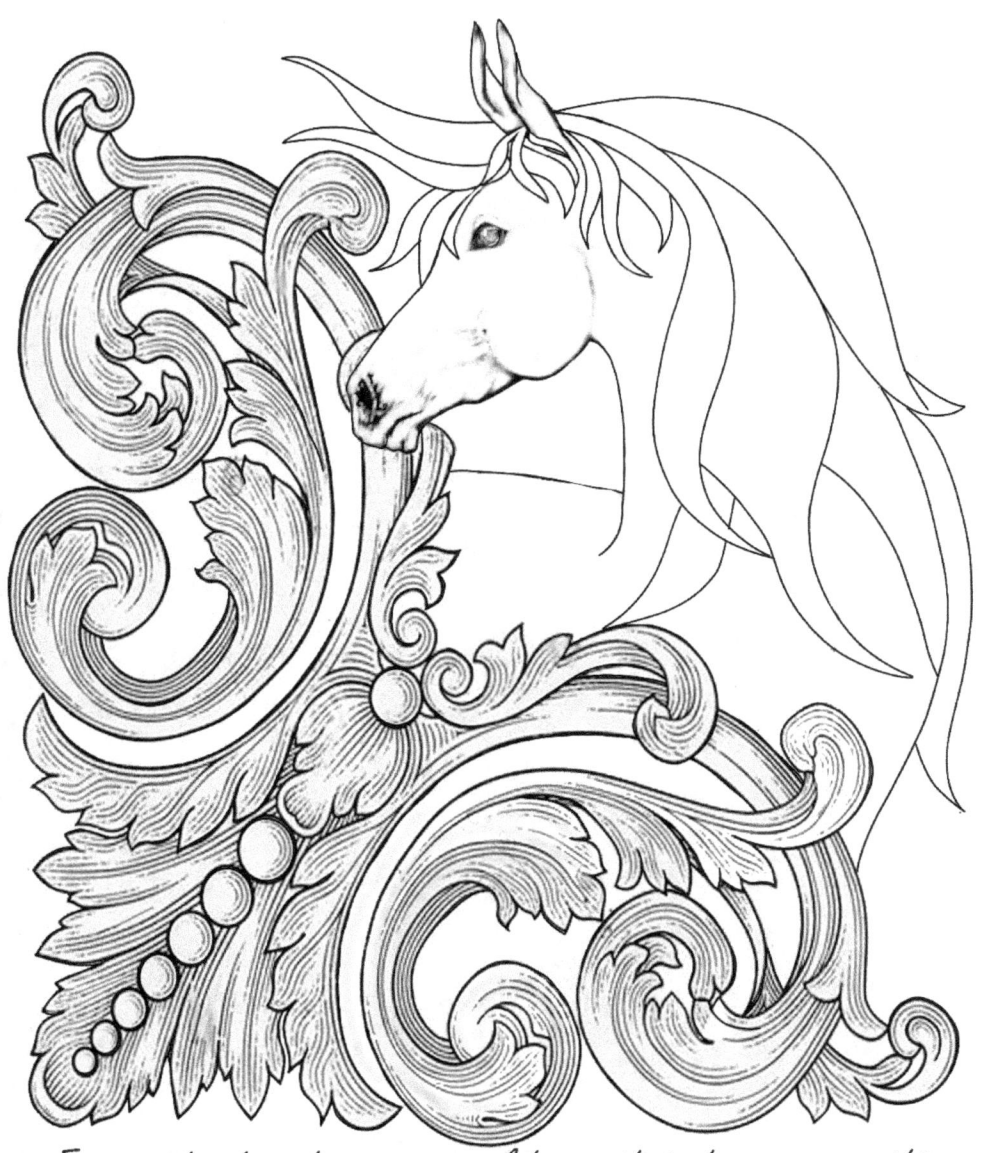

Every rider has that one special horse that changes everything about them, making them greater than they knew they could be.

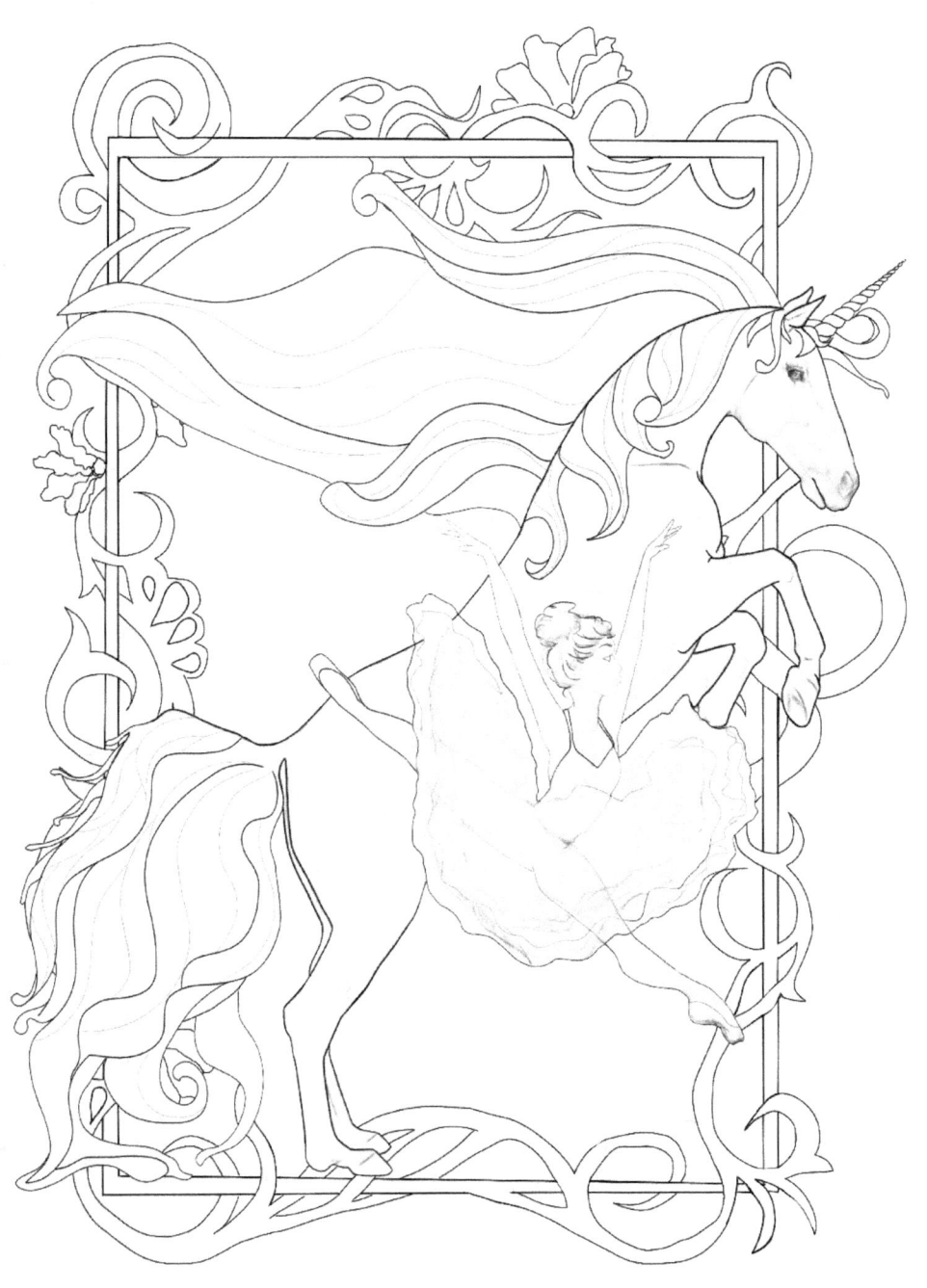

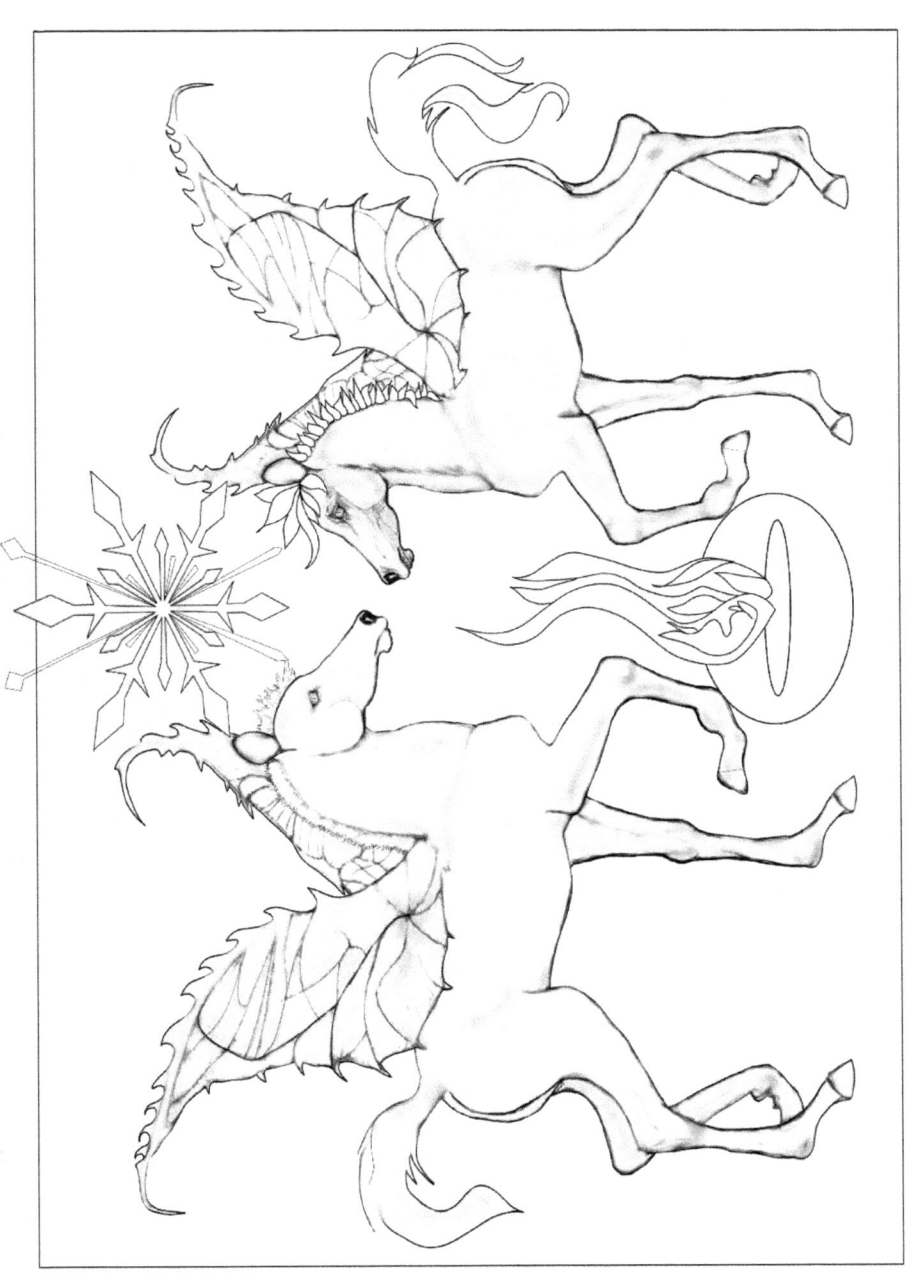

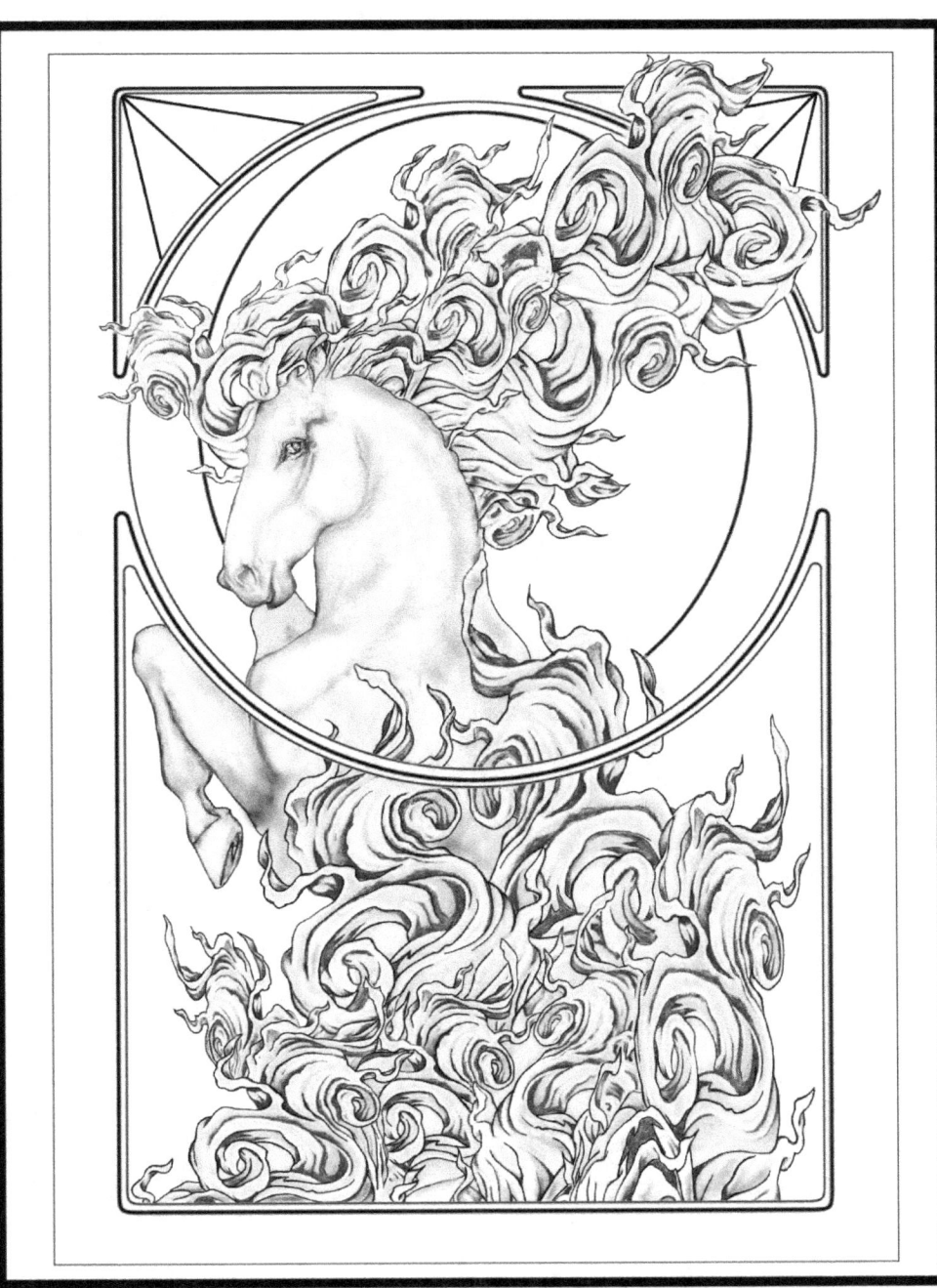

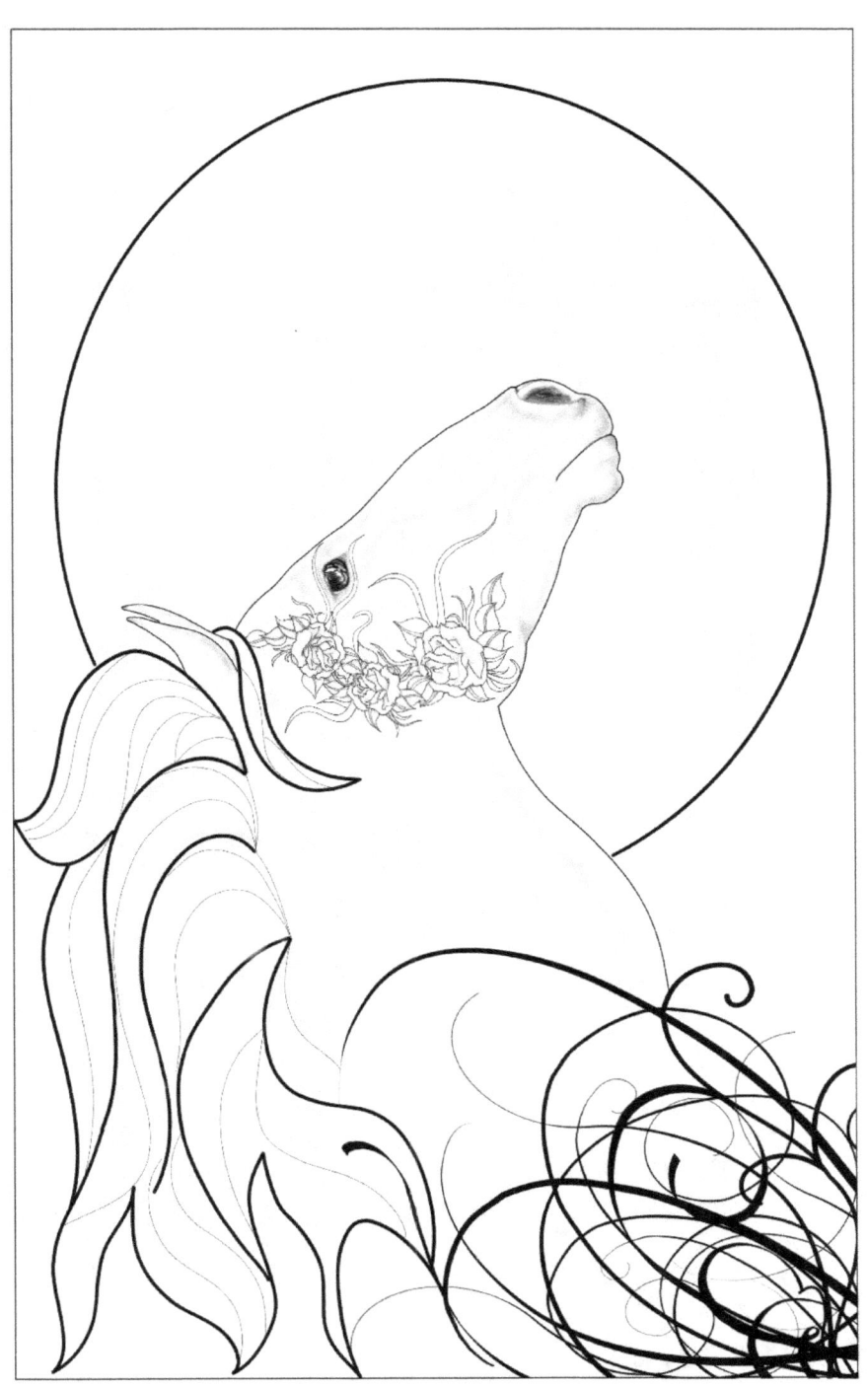

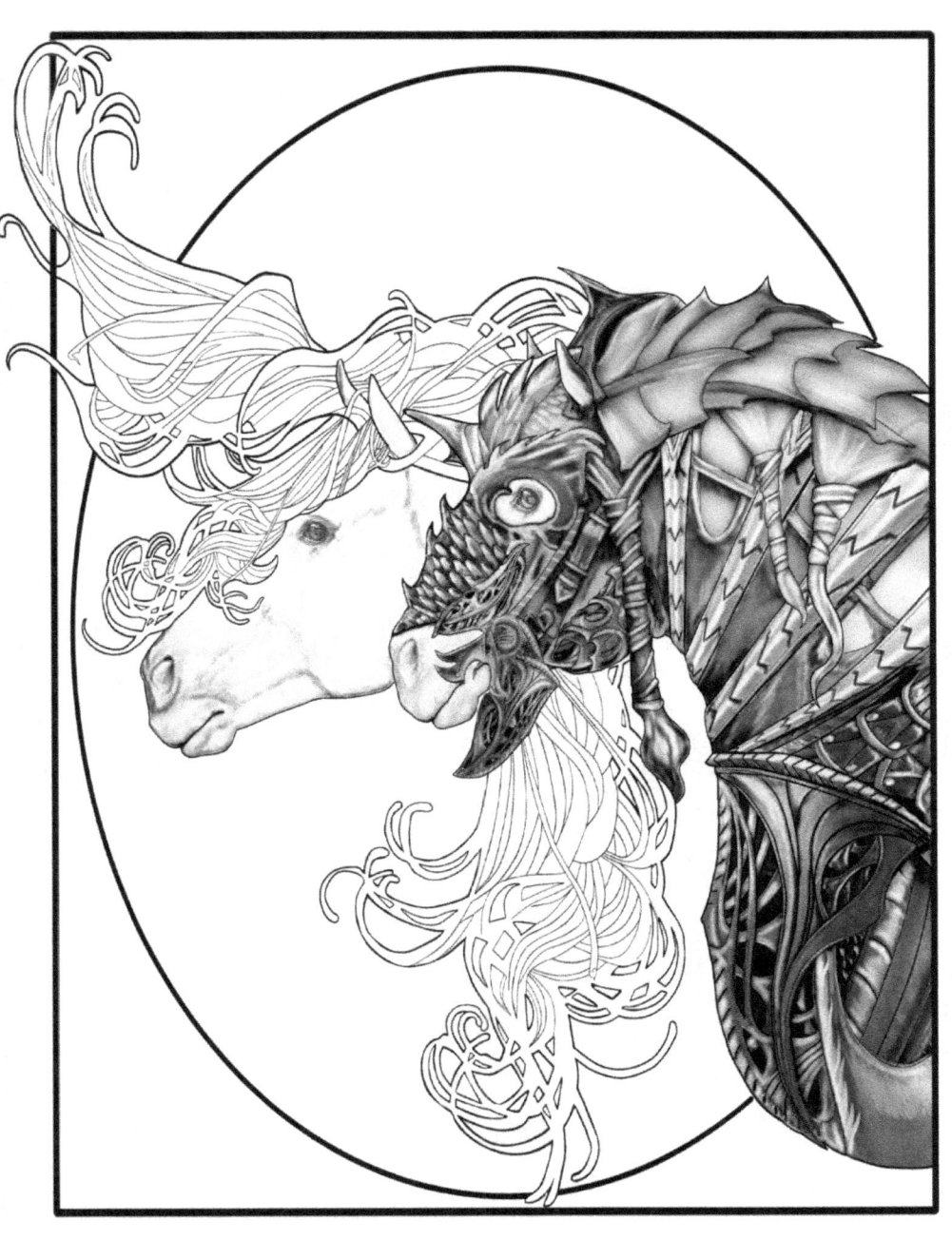

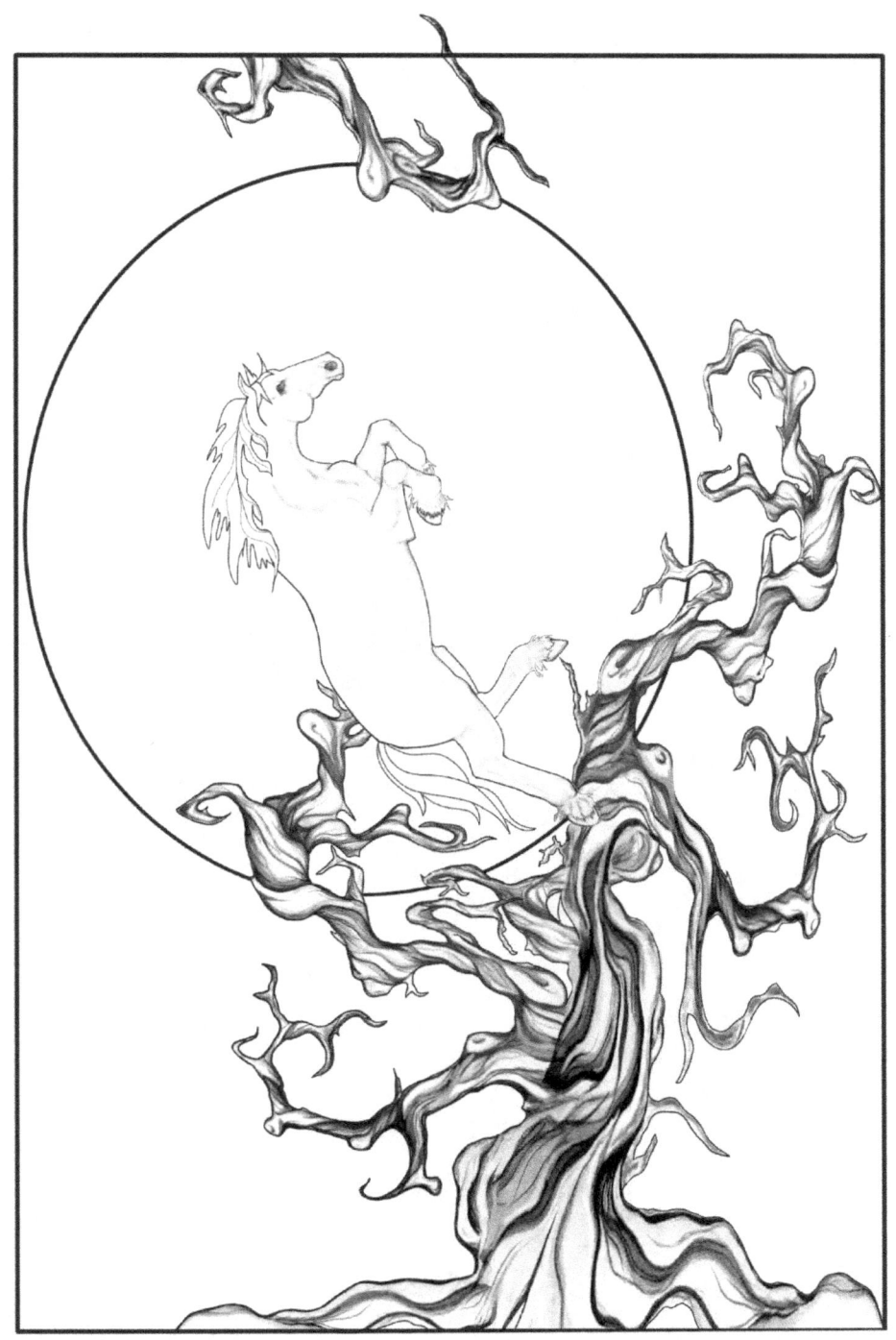

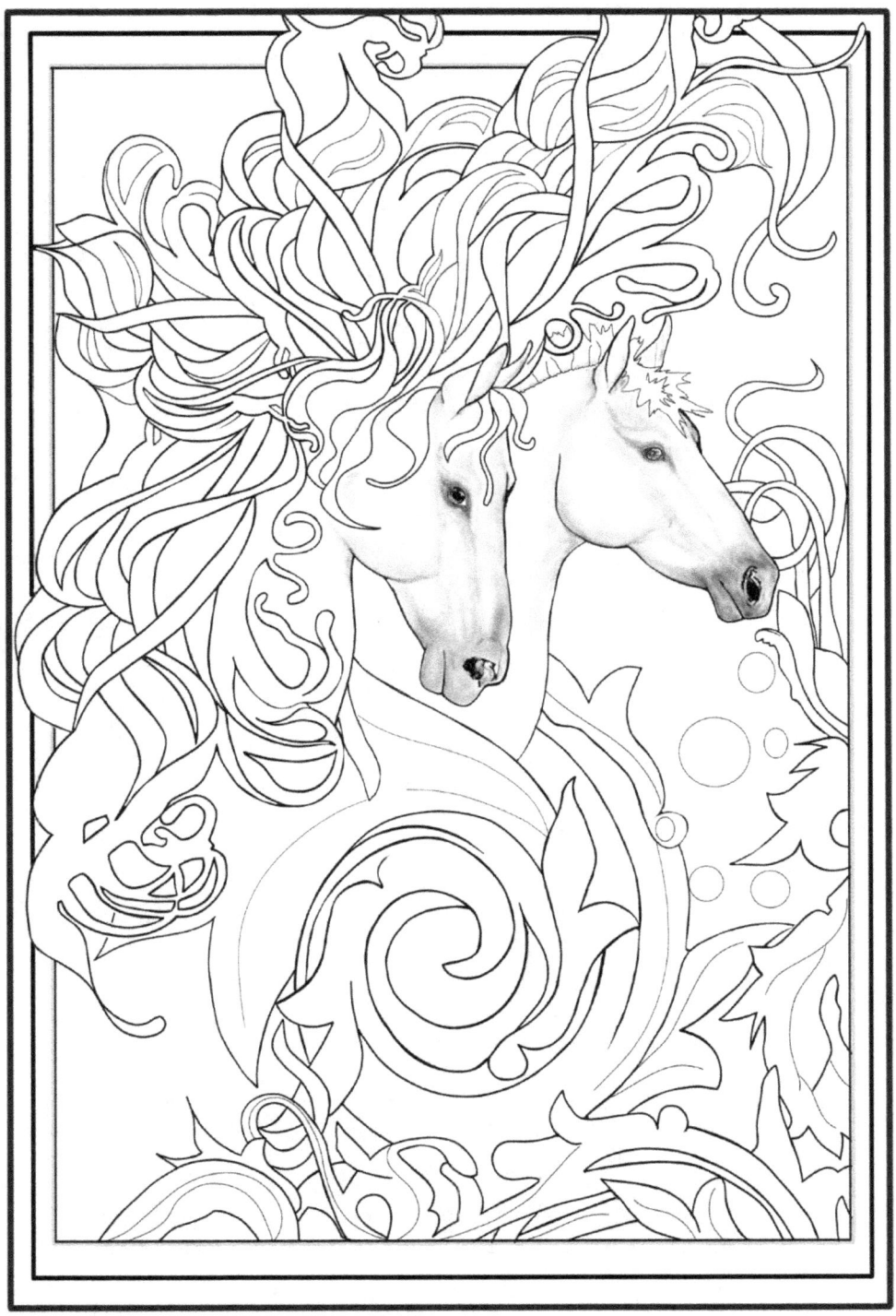

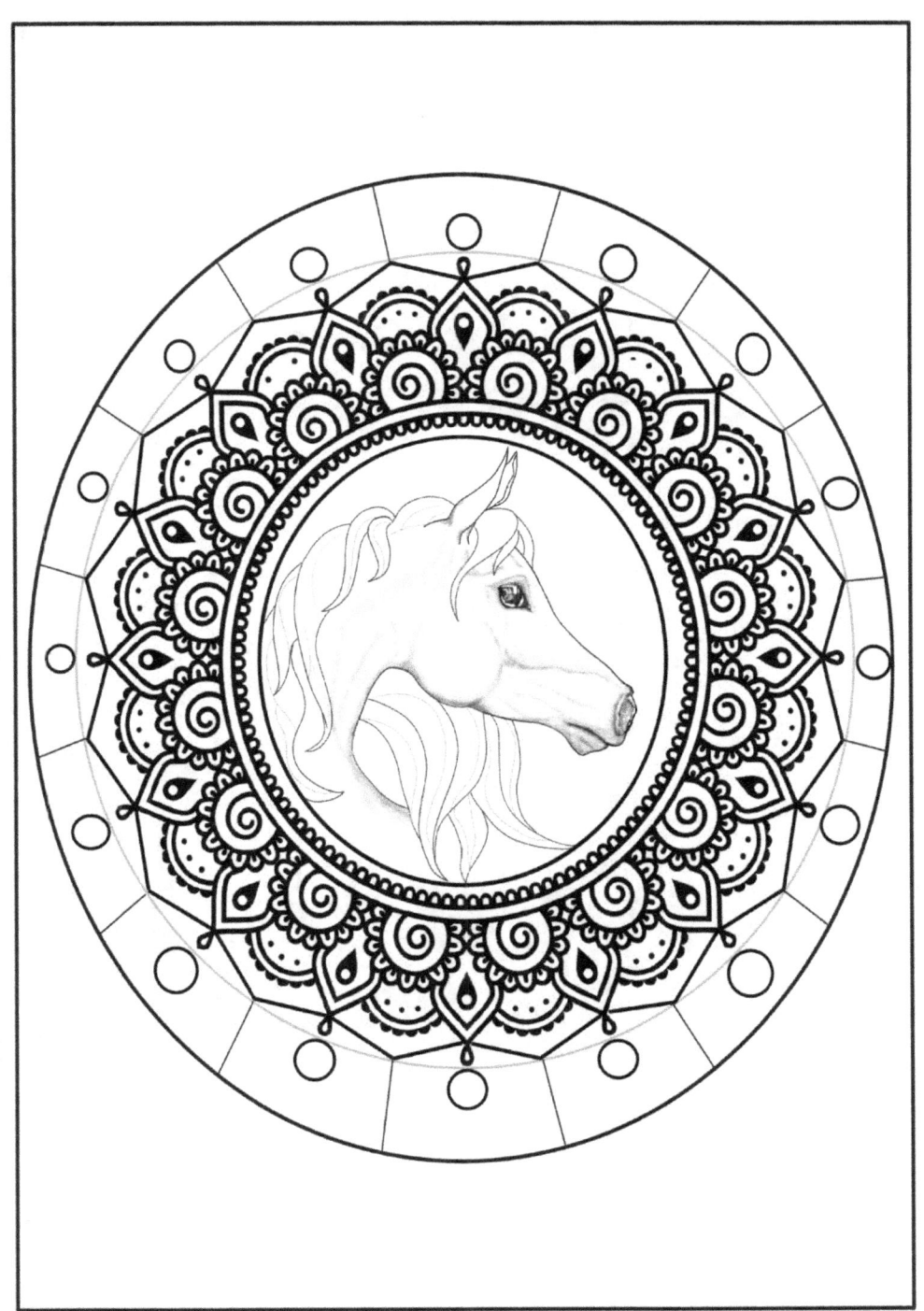

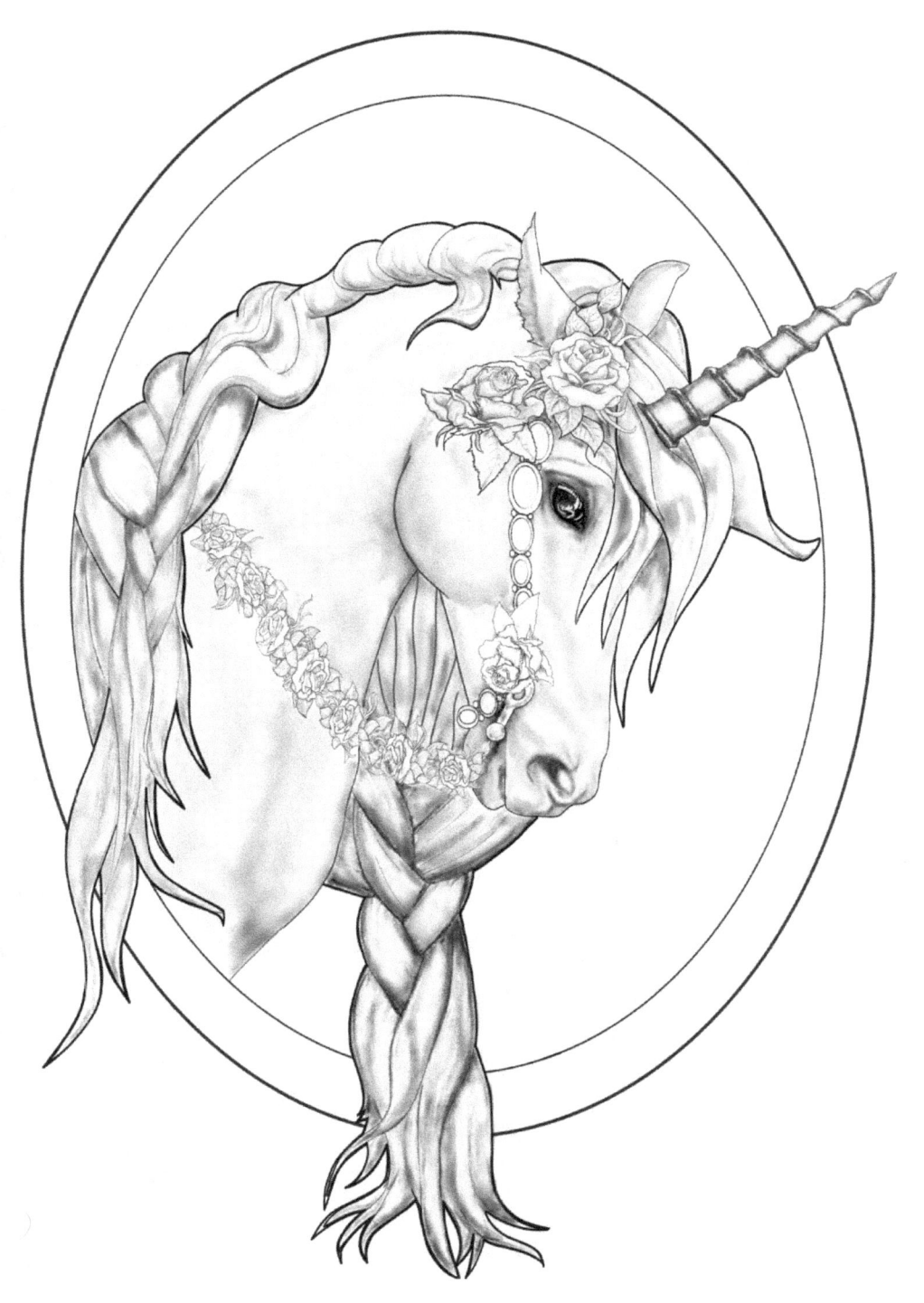

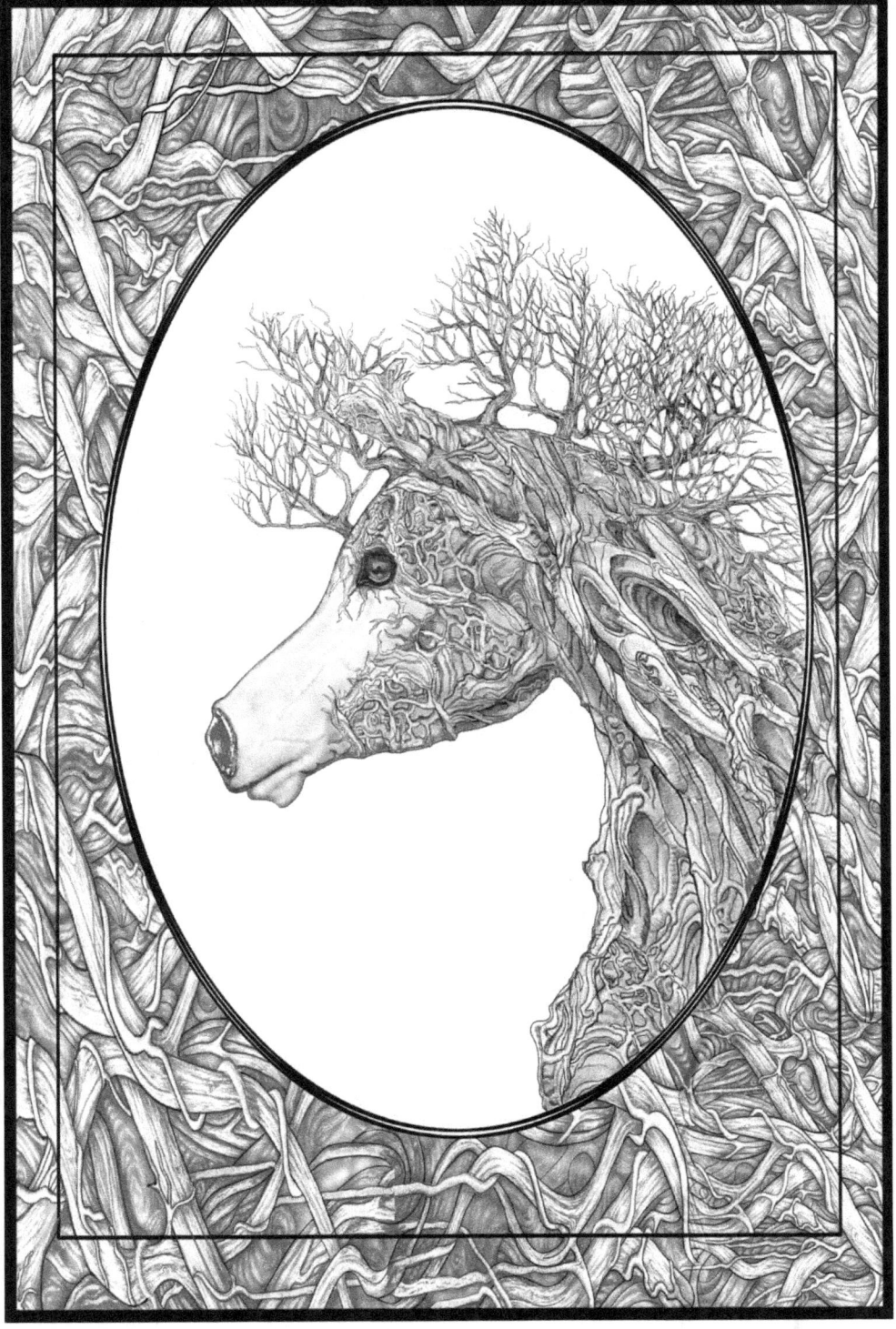

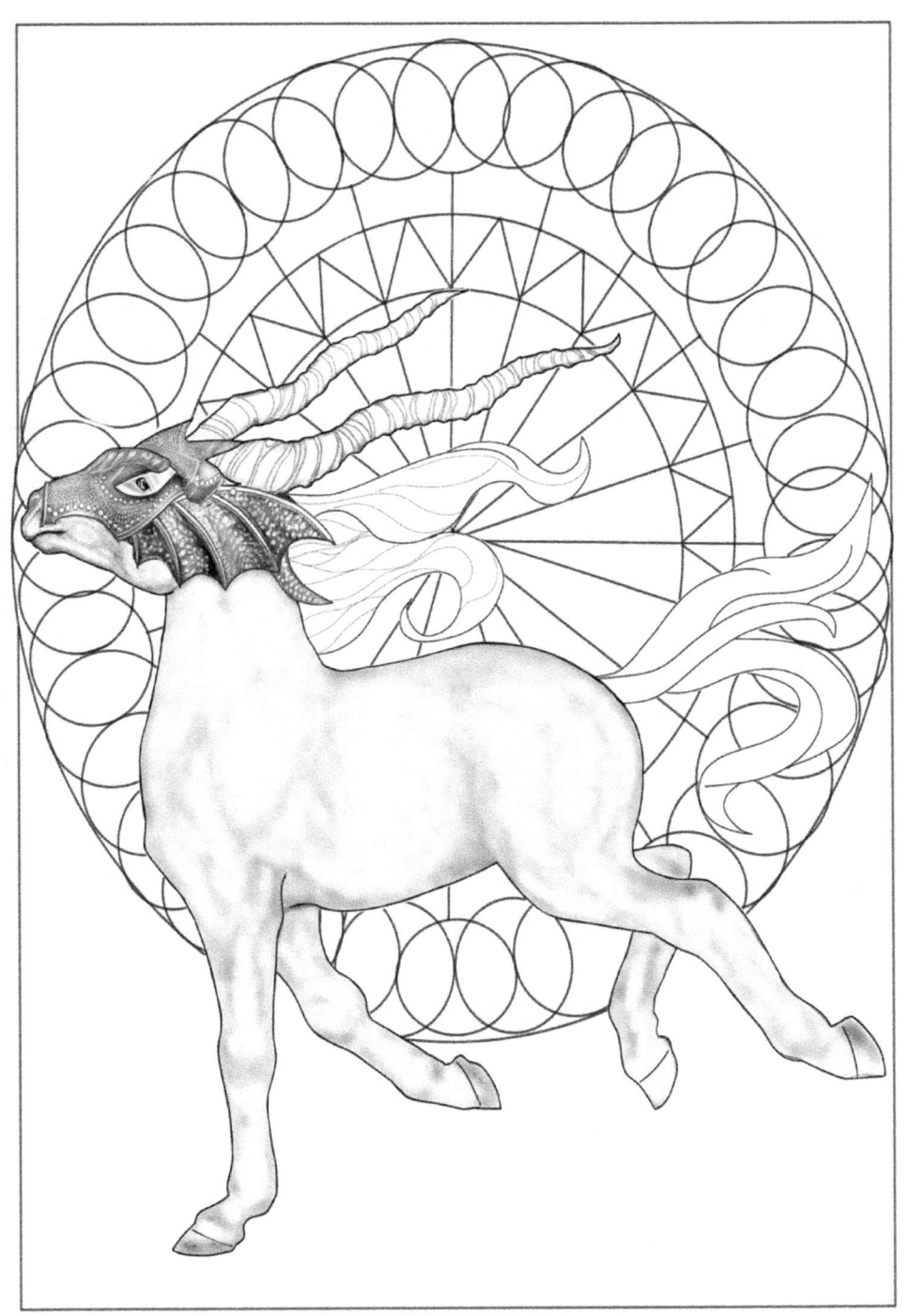

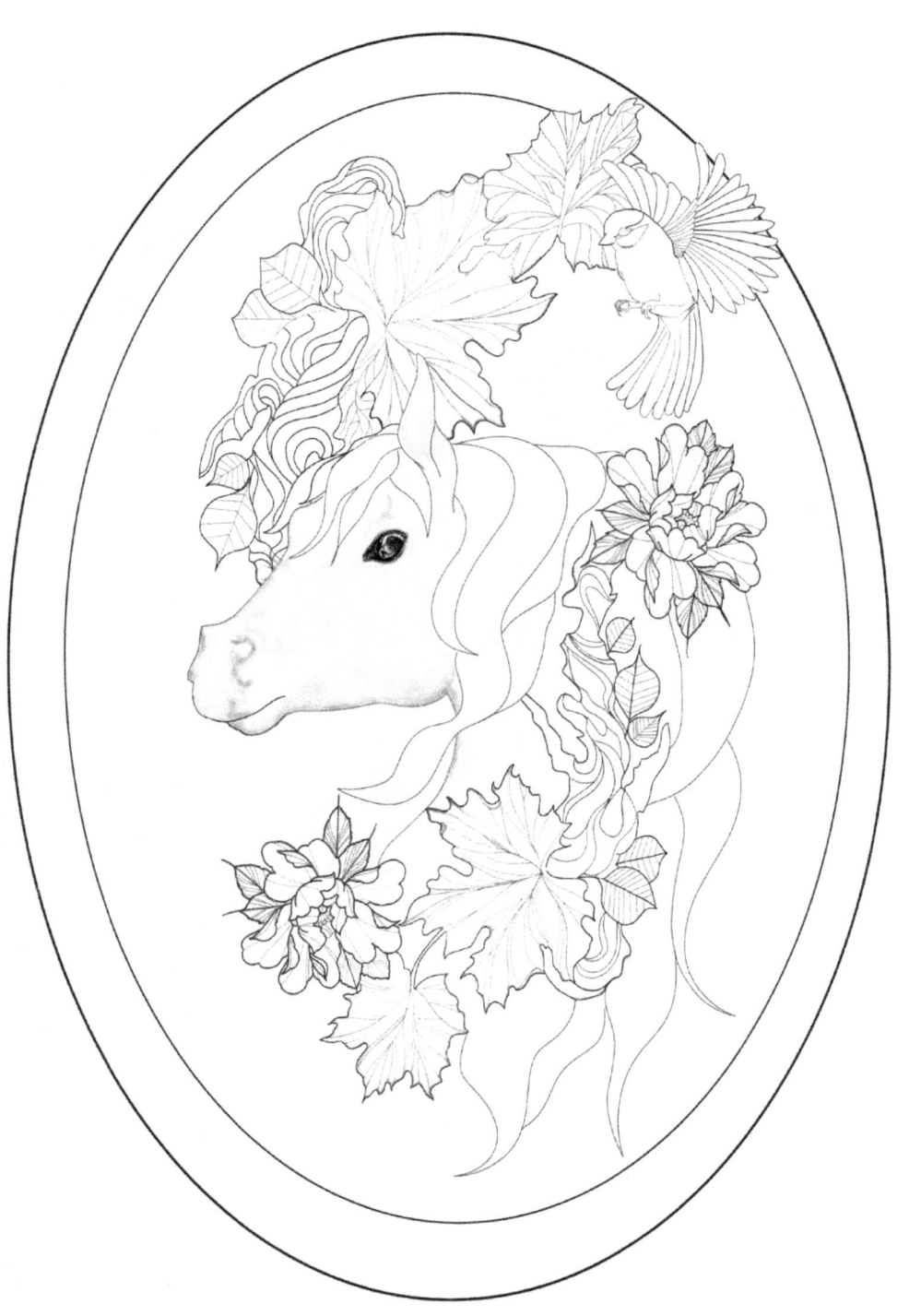

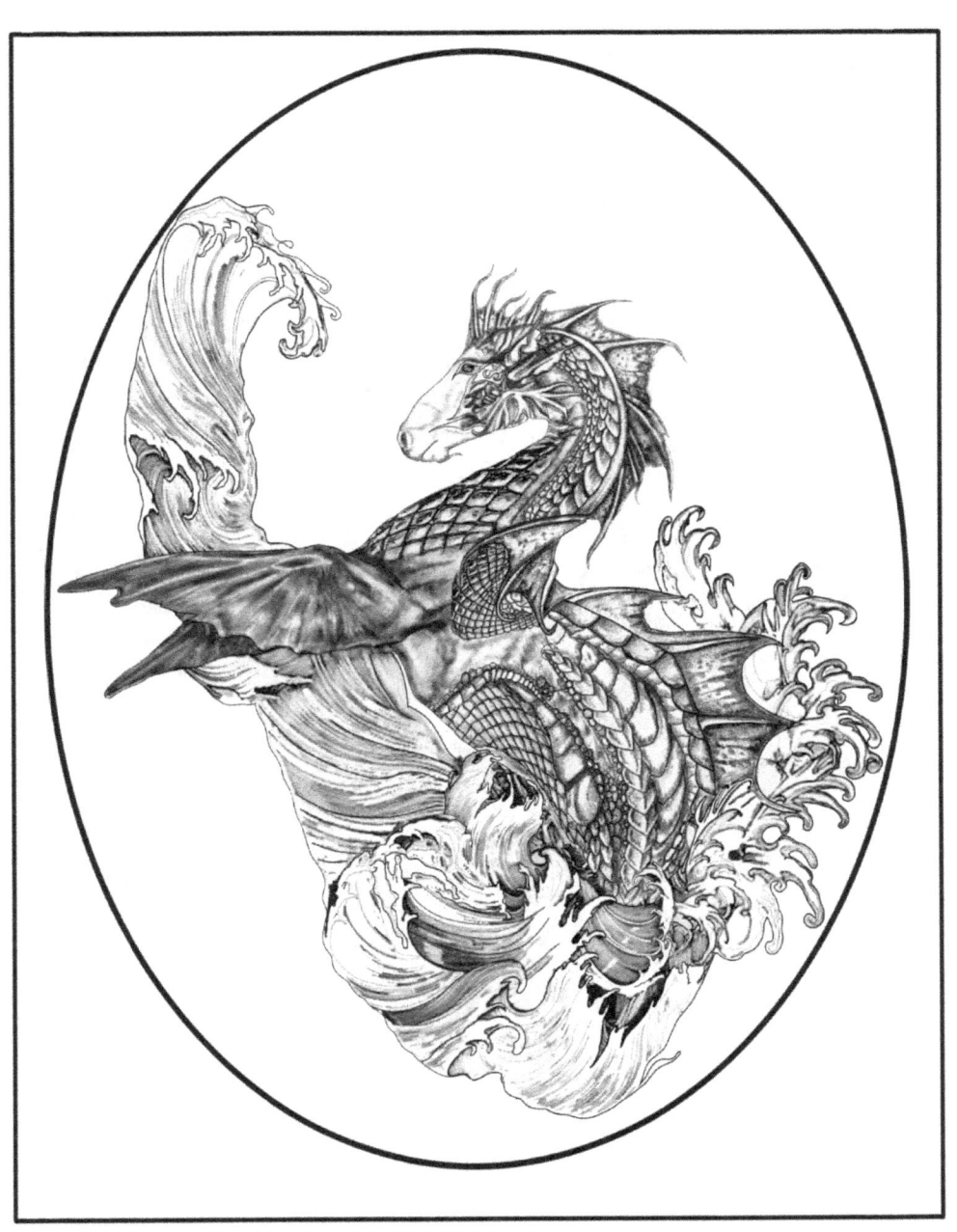

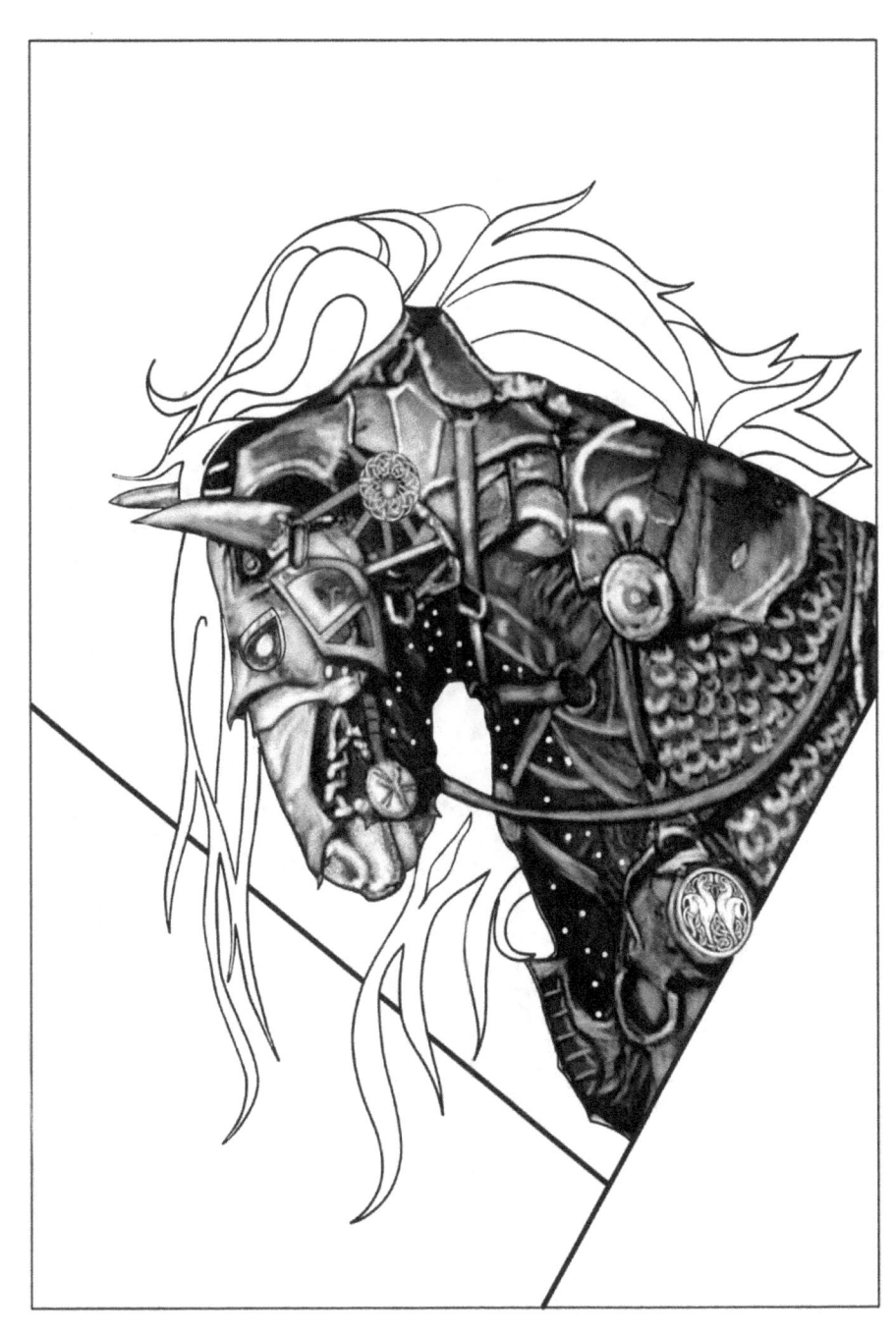

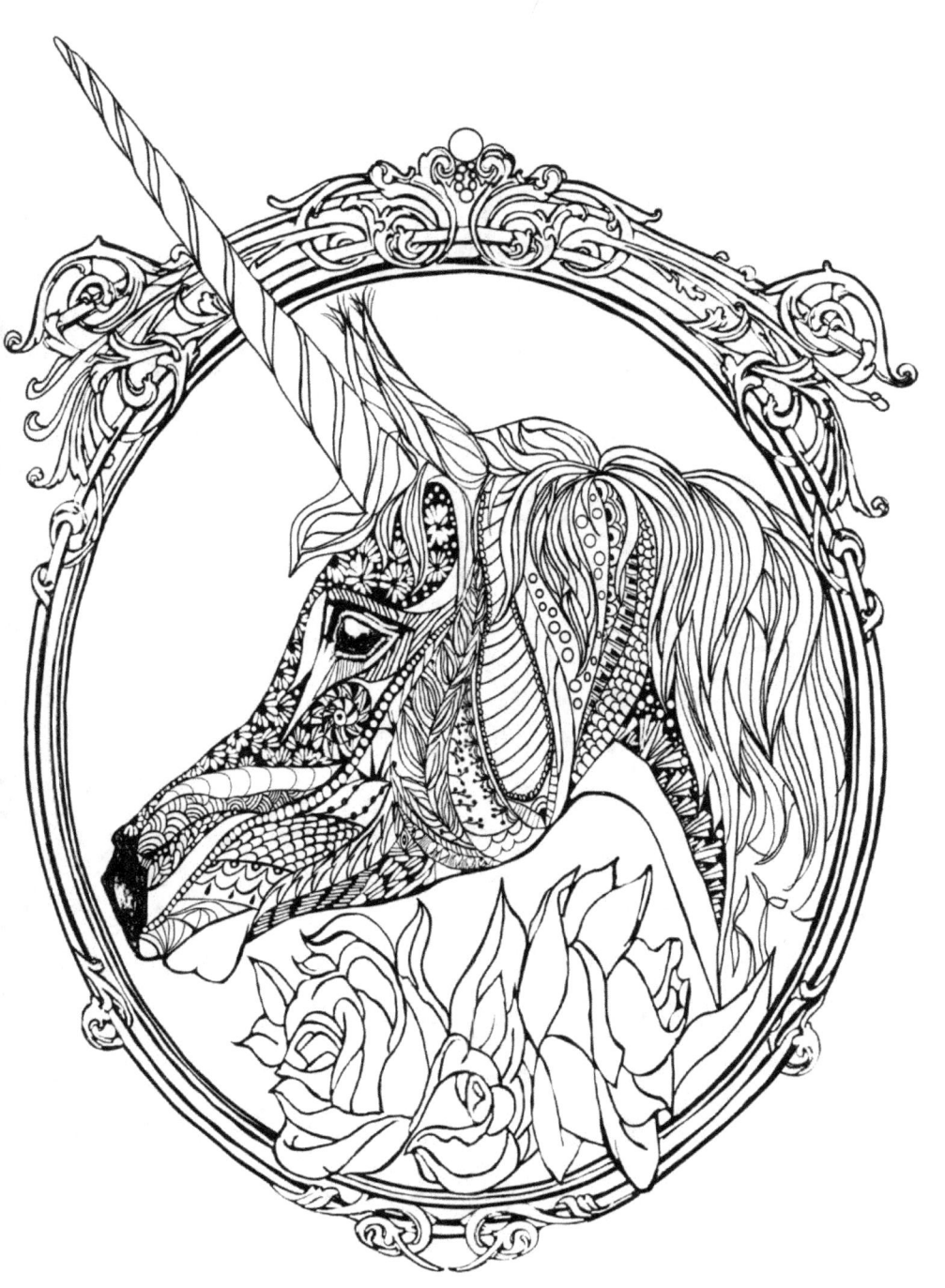

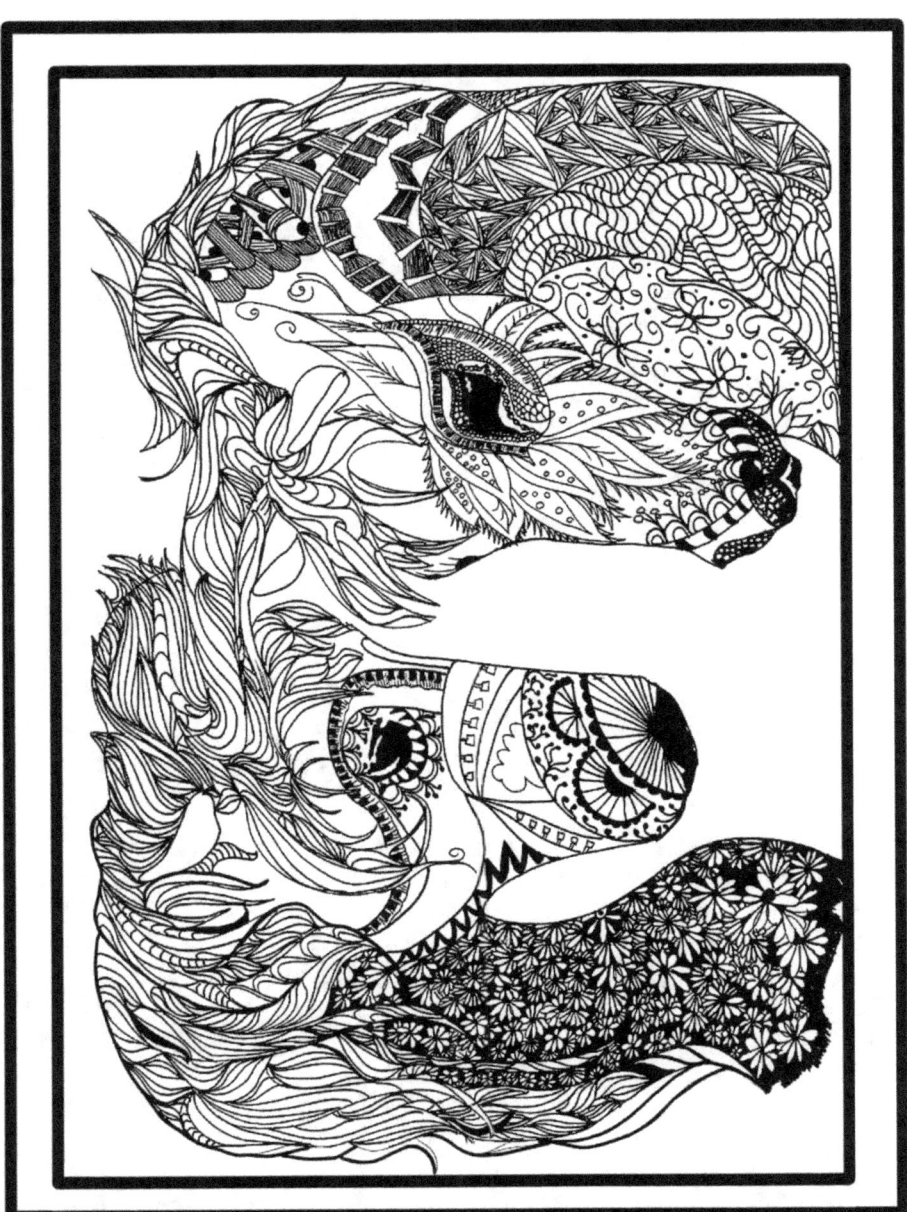

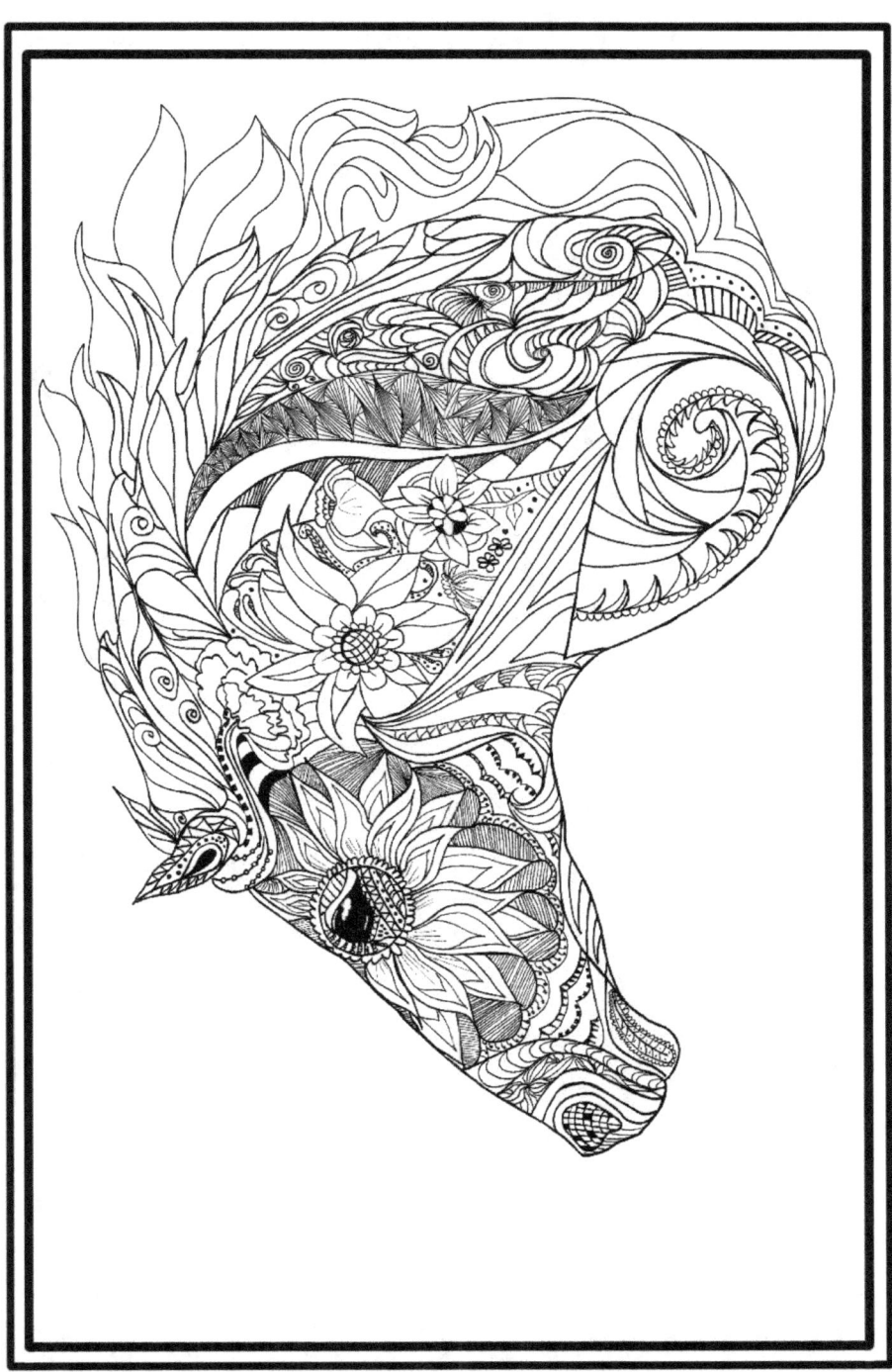

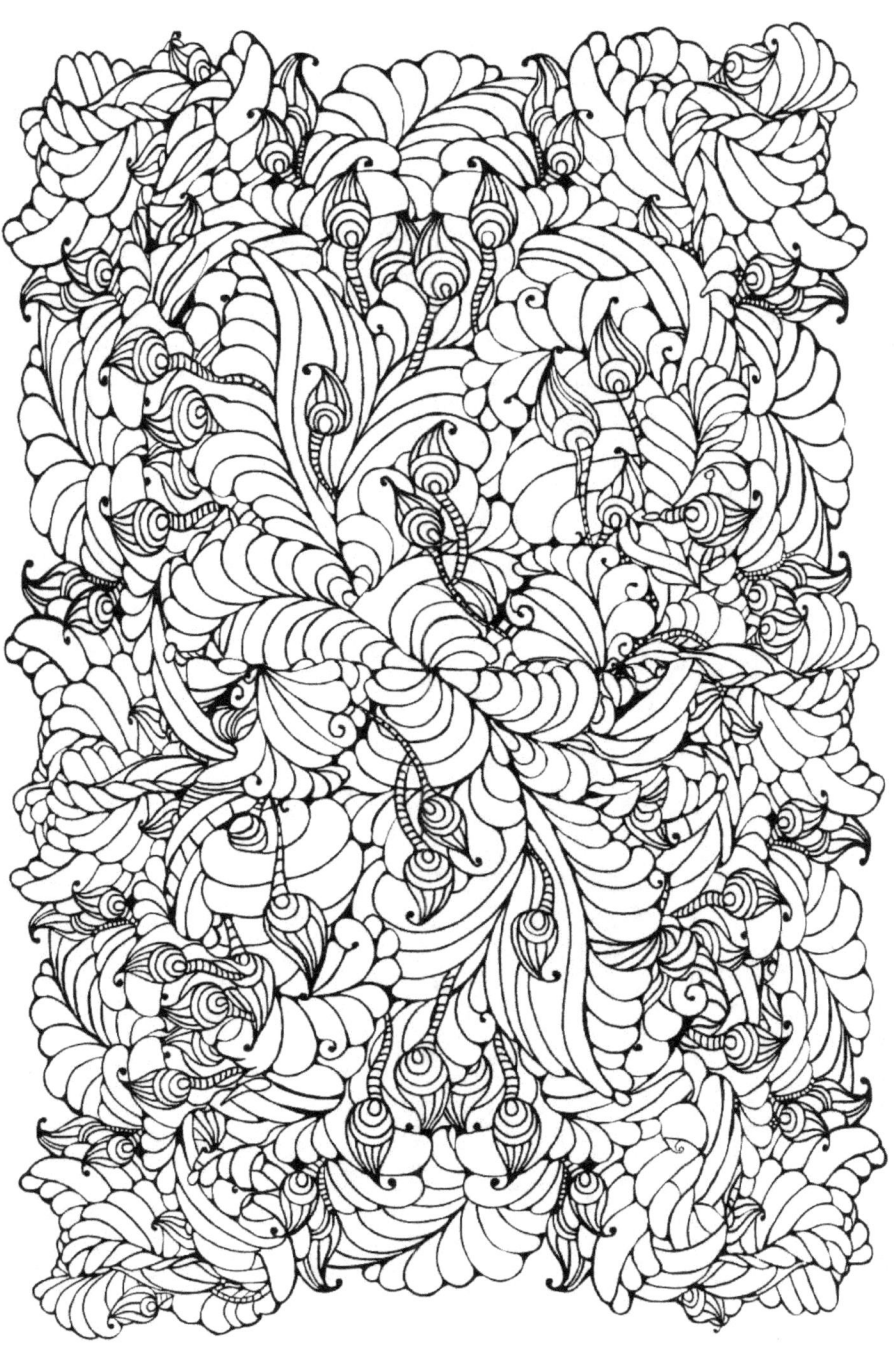

www.ingramcontent.com/pod-product-compliance
Lightning Source LLC
Chambersburg PA
CBHW071201240526
45470CB00017B/1104